water
b ugs &
dragonflies

Water Bugs and
Dragonflies

Explaining Death to
Young Children

water
bugs

Doris Stickney

Illustrations by
Gloria Ortiz Hernandez

continuum

Continuum International Publishing Group

The Tower Building, 11 York Road, London, SE1 7NX

80 Maiden Lane, Suite 704, New York, NY 10038

www.continuumbooks.com

© 1982 and 1997 The Pilgrim Press

Illustrations copyright © 1997 by Gloria Ortiz Hernandez

Adapted from 'Death', *Colloquy*, December 1970.

Copyright 1970 by United Church Press.

First published 1982 by The Pilgrim Press

First published by Mowbray 1984

This revised edition published by Continuum 1997

Reprinted 2010, 2011

British Library Cataloguing-in-Publication Data

A catalogue record for this book is available from the British Library.

ISBN: 978-0-8264-6458-3

Typeset by The Pilgrim Press

Printed and bound in China

water
bugs &
dragonflies

busy scurrying ove

down below the surface of a quiet pond lived a little colony of water bugs. They were a happy colony, living far away from the sun. For many months they were very busy, scurrying over the soft mud on the bottom of the pond.

1

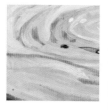

hey did notice that every once in a while one of their colony seemed to lose interest in going about with its friends. Clinging to the stem of a pond lily, it gradually moved out of sight and was seen no more.

"Look!" said one of the water bugs to another. "One of our colony is climbing up the lily stalk. Where do you suppose she is going?"

it went slo

U P,

U P,

U P,

Up, up, up she went slowly. Even as they watched, the water bug disappeared from sight. Her friends waited and waited but she didn't return.

"That's funny!" said one water bug to another.

"Wasn't she happy here?" asked a second water bug.

"Where do you suppose she went?" wondered a third.

No one had an answer. They were greatly puzzled.

"We

finally one of the water bugs, a leader in the colony, gathered his friends together. "I have an idea. The next one of us who climbs up the lily stalk must promise to come back and tell us where he or she went and why."

"We promise," they said solemnly.

promise,"

One spring day, not long after, the very water bug who had suggested the plan found himself climbing up the lily stalk. Up, up, up he went. Before he knew what was happening, he had broken through the surface of the water and fallen onto the broad, green lily pad above. Weary from his journey, he slept.

UP,

UP,

UP,

When he awoke, he looked about with surprise. He couldn't believe what he saw. A startling change had come to his old body. His movement revealed four silver wings and a long tail. Even as he struggled, he felt an impulse to move his wings. The warmth of the

He had becom

sun soon dried the moisture from the new body. He moved his wings again and suddenly found himself up above the water. He had become a dragonfly.

Swooping and dipping in great curves, he flew through the air. He felt exhilarated in the new atmosphere.

dragonfly.

by and by, the new dragonfly lighted happily on a lily pad to rest. Then it was that he chanced to look below to the bottom of the pond. Why, he was right above his old friends, the water bugs! There they were, scurrying about, just as he had been doing some time before.

Then the dragonfly remembered the promise: "The next one of us who climbs up the lily stalk will come back and tell where he or she went and why."

Without thinking, the dragonfly darted down. Suddenly he hit the surface of the water and bounced away. Now that he was a dragonfly, he could no longer go into the water.

"I *can't* return!" he said in dismay.
"I tried, but I can't keep my promise.
Even if I could go back, not one of the
water bugs would know me in my new
body. I guess I'll just have to wait until
they become dragonflies too. Then
they'll understand what happened to
me and where I went."

Wait until the

ecome dragonflies

15

And the dragonfly winged off happily into its wonderful new world of sun and air.

A Prayer

Thank you, God, for the story of the water bugs and the dragonflies. Thank you for the miracle that makes shiny dragonflies out of plain bugs.

Please remember _____, who has left the pond we live in. Give (her/him) a good life too, in a wonderful new world of sun and air.

And then remember me, and let me someday be with (her/him).

Amen.

What Can Parents Say?

Your children's world is full of friends, both people and pets. Then suddenly one is taken by death. Almost every day to some parent or teacher comes the question, "Where has Bobby gone?"

Somehow the answers of an earlier generation now have a hollow sound. Our parents replied, "He has gone to heaven" or "He has gone to be with God." Today's children live in a world of scientific excursions into the heavens. Their vocabulary has grown from watching TV and using computers. "Heaven" to them is not the same as the heaven of our childhood. The old answers will not satisfy today's children.

Nor is anyone ever prepared for tragedy. Such was the case in our little community. Our five-year-old son and his playmate, Bobby, were inseparable companions. Full of energy, they played games or took turns on a neighbor's swing. We loved to see them together.

One summer afternoon as Bobby was swinging, the crosspiece holding the ropes fell. It struck the little boy a crushing blow, taking his life in an instant.

We parents of the neighborhood were terribly shaken. Of course death had entered our lives before. It was not a new experience for any one of us. But what could we say to our children in answer to the inevitable questions? We had to find words that would not only satisfy them but make sense to our own adult minds as well.

It fell to my husband, as pastor of the church, to hold the service in memory of Bobby. In preparing what he should say, he recalled a boyhood experience.

"When I was only nine years old," he said to me, "our minister told the fable of the water bug who changed into a dragonfly. I haven't the slightest idea where the story came from. But the fact that I have remembered it all these years makes me think that I should tell it at Bobby's service. It might be helpful to the parents and the children there."

"Tell me the story again," I urged, "and say how you think we parents could follow it up."

So he began, "Down below the surface of a quiet pond . . . ," and on through to the end of the tale.

"So," he concluded, "any parent or teacher whose child asks, 'Where has Bobby gone?,' will find in the fable the background for easy conversation.

For instance, just imagine our Ned, hearing the story of the water bugs, asking us that very question.

"'We don't really know where Bobby has gone' is our answer. But you remember in the story of the water bugs down in the pool they asked the same question of one another.

"'Tell me,' we might ask Ned in turn, 'why couldn't the dragonfly come back to the water bugs, as he had promised?'

"'Why, of course he couldn't come back. He *couldn't!,*' I'm sure Ned would say. 'You know that. He had another kind of body. His wings were made to fly in the air.'

"Then we would ask, 'What did the dragonfly say when he realized he couldn't go back?'—wondering if Ned had caught the important words.

" 'I'll have to wait until they become dragonflies too. Then they'll understand what happened to me and where I went,' Ned might repeat, remembering the end of the story."

I was profoundly moved by our conversation.

"Don't we as parents have a priceless opportunity to witness to our faith?" I asked. "The fact enters naturally into place that the change in our bodies, which we call death, will come to each of us, sometime. But we believe that *then* we will learn the secret that the dragonfly discovered: God has a plan for all creatures, more wonderful than we could ever imagine."

No one can predict the reaction of children to a story. The world of imagination is more real to them than the visible one. They surprise us with their clear grasp of that which we would make complex. And with unerring honesty, they see through our flimsy pretenses. "I don't know" is an honest admission. But "I believe" gives our children confidence in a future to be anticipated and in a Creator whose plan can be trusted.